Italian Short Stories for Beginners
Book 3

Over 100 Dialogues and Daily Used Phrases to Learn Italian in Your Car. Have Fun & Grow Your Vocabulary, with Crazy Effective Language Learning Lessons

www.LearnLikeNatives.com

www.LearnLikeNatives.com

© **Copyright 2020**
By Learn Like A Native

ALL RIGHTS RESERVED

No part of this book may be reproduced, stored in a retrieval system, or transmitted in any form or by any means, without the prior written permission of the publisher.

www.LearnLikeNatives.com

TABLE OF CONTENT

INTRODUCTION	5
CHAPTER 1 The Car / emotions	17
Translation of the Story	37
The Car	37
CHAPTER 2 Going to A Meeting / telling time	49
Translation of the Story	68
Going to A Meeting	68
CHAPTER 3 Lunch with The Queen / to be, to have + food	79
Translation of the Story	99
Lunch with The Queen	99
CONCLUSION	111
About the Author	117

www.LearnLikeNatives.com

www.LearnLikeNatives.com

INTRODUCTION

Before we dive into some Italian, I want to congratulate you, whether you're just beginning, continuing, or resuming your language learning journey. Here at Learn Like a Native, we understand the determination it takes to pick up a new language and after reading this book, you'll be another step closer to achieving your language goals.

As a thank you for learning with us, we are giving you free access to our 'Speak Like a Native' eBook. It's packed full of practical advice and insider tips on how to make language learning quick, easy, and most importantly, enjoyable. Head over to LearnLikeNatives.com to access your free guide and peruse our huge selection of language learning resources.

Learning a new language is a bit like cooking—you need several different ingredients and the right technique, but the end result is sure to be delicious. We created this book of short stories for learning Italian because language is alive. Language is about the senses—hearing, tasting the words on your tongue, and touching another culture up close. Learning a language in a classroom is a fine place to start, but it's not a complete introduction to a language.

In this book, you'll find a language come to life. These short stories are miniature immersions into the Italian language, at a level that is perfect for beginners. This book is not a lecture on grammar. It's not an endless vocabulary list. This book is the closest you can come to a language immersion without leaving the country. In the stories within, you will see people speaking to each other, going through daily life situations, and using the most common, helpful words and phrases in language.

You are holding the key to bringing your Italian studies to life.

Made for Beginners

We made this book with beginners in mind. You'll find that the language is simple, but not boring. Most of the book is in the present tense, so you will be able to focus on dialogues, root verbs, and understand and find patterns in subject-verb agreement.

This is not "just" a translated book. While reading novels and short stories translated into Italian is a wonderful thing, beginners (and even novices) often run into difficulty. Literary licenses and complex sentence structure can make reading in your second language truly difficult—not to mention BORING. That's why Italian Short

Stories for Beginners is the perfect book to pick up. The stories are simple, but not infantile. They were not written for children, but the language is simple so that beginners can pick it up.

The Benefits of Learning a Second Language

If you have picked up this book, it's likely that you are already aware of the many benefits of learning a second language. Besides just being fun, knowing more than one language opens up a whole new world to you. You will be able to communicate with a much larger chunk of the world. Opportunities in the workforce will open up, and maybe even your day-to-day work will be improved.

Improved communication can also help you expand your business. And from a neurological perspective, learning a second language is like taking your daily vitamins and eating well, for your brain!

How To Use The Book

The chapters of this book all follow the same structure:

- A short story with several dialogs
- A summary in Italian
- A list of important words and phrases and their English translation
- Questions to test your understanding
- Answers to check if you were right
- The English translation of the story to clear every doubt

www.LearnLikeNatives.com

You may use this book however is comfortable for you, but we have a few recommendations for getting the most out of the experience. Try these tips and if they work for you, you can use them on every chapter throughout the book.

1) Start by reading the story all the way through. Don't stop or get hung up on any particular words or phrases. See how much of the plot you can understand in this way. We think you'll get a lot more of it than you may expect, but it is completely normal not to understand everything in the story. You are learning a new language, and that takes time.

2) Read the summary in Italian. See if it matches what you have understood of the plot.

3) Read the story through again, slower this time. See if you can pick up the meaning of any words or phrases you don't understand

by using context clues and the information from the summary.

4) Test yourself! Try to answer the five comprehension questions that come at the end of each story. Write your answers down, and then check them against the answer key. How did you do? If you didn't get them all, no worries!

5) Look over the vocabulary list that accompanies the chapter. Are any of these the words you did not understand? Did you already know the meaning of some of them from your reading?

6) Now go through the story once more. Pay attention this time to the words and phrases you haven't understand. If you'd like, take the time to look them up to expand your meaning of the story. Every time you read over the story, you'll understand more and more.

7) Move on to the next chapter when you are ready.

Read and Listen

The audio version is the best way to experience this book, as you will hear a native Italian speaker tell you each story. You will become accustomed to their accent as you listen along, a huge plus for when you want to apply your new language skills in the real world.

If this has ignited your language learning passion and you are keen to find out what other resources are available, go to LearnLikeNatives.com, where you can access our vast range of free learning materials. Don't know where to begin? An excellent place to start is our 'Speak Like a Native' free eBook, full of practical advice and insider tips on how to make language learning quick, easy, and most importantly, enjoyable.

www.LearnLikeNatives.com

And remember, small steps add up to great advancements! No moment is better to begin learning than the present.

www.LearnLikeNatives.com

FREE BOOK!

Get the *FREE BOOK* that reveals the secrets path to learn any language fast, and without leaving your country.

Discover:

- The **language 5 golden rules** to master languages at will

- Proven **mind training techniques** to revolutionize your learning

- A complete step-by-step guide to **conquering any language**

www.LearnLikeNatives.com

www.LearnLikeNatives.com

www.LearnLikeNatives.com

CHAPTER 1
The Car / emotions

STORIA

Quentin è **interessato** alle auto. Guarda le foto delle auto. Legge sulle auto tutta la notte, ogni notte. Quando **si annoia**, scorre attraverso Instagram. Gli account che segue sono tutti di automobili.

La ragazza di Quentin è Rashel. Rashel è **divertita** dall'ossessione di Quentin. Le auto non le interessano.

Quentin ha una macchina. Quentin guida una Honda Accord 2000. La sua auto è verde. Quentin si sente **imbarazzato** dalla sua auto. Vuole una macchina nuova. Vuole una macchina per guidare in città con Rashel. Sogna belle auto, auto costose. Vuole una grande auto. Lea auto piccole sono noiose.

Ultimamente, Quentin guarda sempre il suo telefono. Quando Rashel lo guarda, Quentin nasconde il telefono.

"Quentin, perché mi nascondi il telefono?" chiede Rashel.

"Per nessuna ragione", dice Quentin.

"Non è vero!" afferma Rashel.

"Te lo prometto!" dice Quentin.

"Fammi vedere lo schermo", prsegue Rashel.

"Non è niente", dice Quentin. "Lascia perdere."

Rashel è **sospettosa**. Quentin sta nascondendo qualcosa.

Una sera, Rashel prepara la cena. Squilla il telefono di Quentin. Lei non conosce il numero. Quentin risponde al telefono.

"Ciao? Oh. Ti chiamo dopo", dice Quentin. Riattacca.

"Chi è?" dice Rashel.

"Nessuno", dice Quentin.

"È una ragazza?" chiede Rashel. È **gelosa**.

"No, non lo è", dice Quentin.

"Allora chi è?" chiede Rashel.

"Nessuno", dice Quentin.

"Perché non me lo dici?" chiede Rashel.

www.LearnLikeNatives.com

È così **arrabbiato**; Quentin esce di casa. Lascia il cibo sul tavolo. Fa freddo. Rashel è **triste**. La cena è stata uno spreco. Rashel chiama il suo amico. Parlano della cena. L'amico di Rashel pensa che Quentin sia con un'altra ragazza. Rashel non ne è convinta. Quentin sta nascondendo qualcosa. È sicura.

Quentin si siede nella sua auto. Apre il suo computer portatile. Cerca annunci per auto di seconda mano. Ci sono auto a buon mercato e auto costose. Lui è **speranzoso**. Cerca una macchina che sia un buon affare. Ha un po' di soldi. Lui e Rashel risparmiano soldi. Li usano per le vacanze. Ma quest'anno, Quentin vuole una macchina, non una vacanza.

Vede un annuncio su una vecchia auto. L'auto è dell'anno 1990. L'auto è una Jeep. Il modello è un Grand Wagoneer. Egli è **curioso** di conoscere l'auto. Nessuna auto assomiglia a questa macchina. Ha del legno all'esterno. Quentin pensa che sia molto bello.

Quentin chiama il numero dell'annuncio.

"Pronto", dice un uomo.

"Salve", dice Quentin. "Chiamo per la macchina."

"Quale macchina?" chiede l'uomo.

"La Jeep", dice Quentin. "La prendo."

"Ok", risponde l'uomo.

"Verrò a prenderla domani", dice Quentin.

"Ok!" dice l'uomo. riaggancia il telefono.

Quentin torna a casa. Si **sente in colpa**. La cena è fredda. La mangia comunque. È nervoso. Cosa penserà Rashel della macchina?

Il giorno dopo, Quentin ottiene la macchina. Quentin ama la nuova auto. La sua auto è una Jeep Grand Wagoneer del 1990. È una grande auto. Ha pannelli di legno lungo i lati.

Quentin guida fino a casa. L'auto ha 120.000 chilometri. Ha circa 30 anni. L'auto è in ottime condizioni. Tutto funziona. L'interno è come nuovo. La nuova auto di Quentin è speciale. Non si **vergogna** di guidarla. Al contrario, si sente

orgoglioso di guidare attraverso la città. Cosa c'è da non amare?

Bussa alla porta. Rashel la apre.

"Rashel", dice. "Guarda!" Quentin indica la macchina.

"Hai una macchina nuova?" chiede.

"Sì," dice Quentin. E invita Rashel a guidare. I due guidare intorno alla città. Quentin guida lentamente. Molte persone fissano l'auto. E 'una macchina speciale. Diversi uomini sembrano **invidiosi**. Vogliono una macchina forte. Quentin è finalmente **felice**.

Quentin passa ogni giorno con la Jeep. La guida. A volte non va in un posto preciso. Gira solo per la città. Ama la sua macchina. **Ha fiducia** nella sua Jeep. Passa ogni sera a pulire la macchina. Lucida le porte e le finestre ogni sera. Rashel lo aspetta. È in ritardo per la cena. Questo **fa infuriare** Rashel. Lei odia la Jeep Wagoneer. Lei pensa che Quentin ami la macchina più di quanto ami lei. Lei ne parla con Quentin e lui le dice di non essere **stupido**. Lui le dà un abbraccio **d'amore**. Vuole mostrarle che si sbaglia.

Sabato, Rashel e Quentin vanno al supermercato. È Quentin che guida. I finestrini sono abbassati. Quentin indossa occhiali da sole. Sembra **sicuro di sé**. Parcheggia l'auto. I due vanno al supermercato.

Fanno la spesa per la frutta.

"Quentin, puoi prendere quattro mele?" chiede Rashel. Quentin va a prendere il frutto. Ritorna. Ma ha quattro arance.

"Quentin, ho detto mele!" dice Rashel.

"Sì, lo so", dice Quentin.

"Queste sono arance!" dice Rashel.

"Oh, scusa", dice Quentin. È **distratto**. Non riesce a concentrarsi.

"Cosa c'è che non va?" chiede Rashel.

"Niente", dice Quentin.

"A cosa stai pensando?" chiede lei.

"A niente", dice Quentin. Ha uno sguardo **ansioso**. Ha uno sguardo **preoccupato**.

"Stai pensando alla macchina?" chiede Rashel.

"No", dice Quentin.

"Sì invece! Lo so! Vai a prendermi delle mele", dice Rashel. Lei è **determinata** a far prestare attenzione a Quentin. Quentin riporta le mele. Le mette nel carrello. Finiscono di fare la spesa. Quentin è silenzioso. Sembra **chiuso in sé stesso**. Vanno alla macchina.

www.LearnLikeNatives.com

Il parcheggio è pieno. Quentin ispeziona la jeep con attenzione. **Ha paura** di segni o graffi. Una portiera lascia segni quando colpisce un'altra portiera. Ci sono molte auto ora. Non vede nessun graffio. Quentin apre la macchina. Entra.

Rashel mette la spesa in macchina. Lei riporta il carrello al negozio. Apre la porta ed entra.

"Quentin, sono **infelice**", dice. Sta piangendo.

"Cosa?" dice Quentin. È **sorpreso**. "Cosa c'è che non va?"

"Ti importa solo della macchina", dice Rashel.

"Non è vero", dice Quentin.

"Tu non mi aiuti a fare niente", dice Rashel.

"Sì! Ci tengo a te", dice Quentin.

"Se ci tieni a me, vendi questa macchina!", conclude Rashel.

RIASSUNTO

Quentin vuole una macchina nuova. Nasconde la sua ricerca alla sua ragazza Rashel. Lei gli chiede chi gli telefona. E gli chiede cosa sta guardando. Ma Quentin mantiene la sua ricerca un segreto. Quentin trova una macchina che ama. Egli è finalmente felice. Tuttavia, è troppo ossessionato con la sua macchina. Rashel diventa gelosa. Quentin non riesce a concentrarsi al negozio di alimentari. Egli è preoccupato che qualcuno graffi l'auto. Quentin non aiuta Rashel con la spesa. Lei si arrabbia, e dice a Quentin che deve scegliere tra lei e la macchina.

LISTA DI VOCABOLI

Interessato	interested
Annoiato	bored
Divertita	amused
Sospettoso	suspicious
Imberazzato /vergognarsi	embarrassed
Gelsoso	jealous

Arrabbiato	angry
Triste	sad
Speranzoso	hopeful
Curioso	curious
Sentirsi in colpa	guilty
Nervoso	nervous
Vergognarsi	ashamed
Orgoglioso	proud
Invidioso	envious
Felice	happy
Infuriato	enraged

Stupido	stupid
D'amore	loving
Fiducioso	confident
Distratto	distracted
Ansioso	anxious
Preoccupato	worried
Determinato	determined
Chiuso in se stesso	withdrawn
Infelice	miserable
Sorpreso	surprised

DOMANDE

1) Cosa pensa Quentin della sua auto all'inizio della storia?

    a) la ama

    b) ne è imbarazzato

    c) è troppo nuova

    d) è troppo costosa

2) Perché Rashel si arrabbia a cena?

    a) pensa che una ragazza stia chiamando Quentin

    b) ha fame

    c) Quentin è in ritardo

    d) Quentin ha dimenticato di comprare il pane

3) Cosa fa Quentin al supermercato?

   a) paga per tutto

   b) prende delle arance al posto delle mele

   c) versa il latte

   d) presta attenzione a Rashel

4) Cosa pensa Quentin della sua nuova auto?

   a) è troppo nuova

   b) è troppo piccola

   c) ne è orgoglioso

   d) ne è imbarazzato

5) Alla fine della storia, Quentin e Rashel:

   a) si baciano

b) fanno la lotta

c) lasciano il negozio

d) hanno una discussione

RISPOSTE

1) Cosa pensa Quentin della sua auto all'inizio della storia?

    b) ne è imbarazzato

2) Perché Rashel si arrabbia a cena?

    a) pensa che una ragazza stia chiamando Quentin

3) Cosa fa Quentin al supermercato?

b) prende delle arance al posto delle mele

4) Cosa pensa Quentin della sua nuova auto?

c) ne è orgoglioso

5) Alla fine della storia, Quentin e Rashel:

d) hanno una discussione

www.LearnLikeNatives.com

Translation of the Story

The Car

STORY

Quentin is **interested** in cars. He looks at pictures of cars. He reads about cars all night, every night. When he is **bored**, he scrolls through Instagram. The accounts he follows are all about cars.

Quentin's girlfriend is Rashel. Rashel is **amused** by Quentin's obsession. Cars do not interest her.

Quentin has a car. Quentin drives a 2000 Honda Accord. His car is green. Quentin feels **embarrassed** by his car. He wants a cool car. He wants a car to drive around town with Rashel. He dreams of nice cars, expensive cars. He wants a big car. Small cars are boring.

Lately, Quentin looks at his phone all the time. When Rashel looks at it, Quentin hides the phone.

"Quentin, why do you hide the phone from me?" asks Rashel.

"No reason," says Quentin.

"That's not true!" says Rashel.

"I promise it is!" says Quentin.

"Then let me see the screen," says Rashel.

"It's nothing," says Quentin. "Forget about it."

Rashel is **suspicious**. Quentin is hiding something.

One night, Rashel makes dinner. Quentin's phone rings. She does not know the number. Quentin answers the phone.

"Hello? Oh. I will call you later," says Quentin. He hangs up.

"Who is it?" says Rashel.

"Nobody," says Quentin.

"Is it a girl?" asks Rashel. She is **jealous**.

"No it is not," says Quentin.

"Then who is it?" asks Rashel.

"Nobody," says Quentin.

"Why won't you tell me?" asks Rashel.

He is so **angry**; Quentin walks out of the house. He leaves the food on the table. It gets cold. Rashel is **sad**. The dinner is a waste. Rashel calls her friend. They talk about the dinner. Rashel's friend thinks Quentin is with another girl. Rashel is unsure. Quentin is hiding something. She is sure.

Quentin sits in his car. He opens his laptop. He searches adverts for second-hand cars. There are cheap cars and expensive cars. He is **hopeful**. He looks for a car that is a good bargain. He has a little money. He and Rashel save money. They use it for vacation. This year, Quentin wants a car, not a vacation.

He sees an advert about an old car. The car is from the year 1990. The car is a Jeep. The model is a Grand Wagoneer. He is **curious** about the car. No cars look like this car. It has wood on the outside. Quentin thinks that is cool.

Quentin calls the number on the advert.

"Hello," says a man.

"Hello," says Quentin. "I am calling about the car."

"Which car?" asks the man.

"The Jeep," says Quentin. "I'll take it."

"Ok," says the man.

"I'll come get it tomorrow," says Quentin.

"Ok!" says the man. He hangs up the phone.

Quentin goes back to the house. He feels **guilty**. Dinner is cold. He eats it anyway. He is **nervous**. What will Rashel think about the car?

The next day, Quentin gets the car. Quentin loves the new car. His car is a 1990 Jeep Grand Wagoneer. It is a big car. It has wood panels along the side.

Quentin drives to the house. The car has 120,000 kilometers. It is about 30 years old. The car is in very good condition. Everything works. The interior is like new. Quentin's new car is special. He does not feel **ashamed** driving. On the contrary, he feels **proud** driving through town. What is not to love?

He knocks on the door. Rashel opens it.

"Rashel," he says. "Look!" Quentin points at the car.

"You have a new car?" she asks.

"Yes," says Quentin. He invites Rashel to ride. The two drive around town. Quentin drives slow. Many people stare at the car. It is a special car.

Several men look **envious**. They want a cool car. Quentin is finally **happy**.

Quentin spends every day with the Jeep. He drives it. Sometimes he has nowhere to go. He just drives around town. He loves the car. He feels **confident** in the Jeep. He spends every evening cleaning the car. He polishes the doors and windows every night. Rashel waits for him. He is late for dinner. This makes Rashel **enraged**. She hates the Jeep Wagoneer. She thinks Quentin loves the car more than he loves her. She tells Quentin this and he tells her not to be **stupid**. He gives her a **loving** hug. He wants to show her she is wrong.

On Saturday, Rashel and Quentin go to the supermarket. Quentin drives them. The windows are down. Quentin wears sunglasses. He looks **confident** and sure of himself. He parks the car. The two go into the supermarket.

They shop for fruit.

"Quentin, can you get four apples?" asks Rashel. Quentin goes to get the fruit. He returns. But he has four oranges.

"Quentin, I said apples!" says Rashel.

"Yeah, I know," says Quentin.

"These are oranges!" says Rashel.

"Oh, sorry," says Quentin. He is **distracted**. He cannot concentrate.

"What is wrong?" asks Rashel.

"Nothing," says Quentin.

"What are you thinking about?" she asks.

"Nothing," says Quentin. He has an **anxious** look. He has a **worried** look in his eyes.

"Are you thinking about the car?" asks Rashel.

"No," says Quentin.

"Yes you are! I know it! Go get me some apples," says Rashel. She is **determined** to make Quentin pay attention. Quentin brings back the apples. He puts them in the cart. They finish grocery shopping. Quentin is quiet. He seems **withdrawn**. They go to the car.

The parking lot is full. Quentin inspects the Jeep carefully. He is **afraid** of marks or scratches. A car door leaves marks when it hits another door. There are many cars now. He does not see any scratches. Quentin unlocks the car. He gets in.

Rashel puts the groceries in the car. She returns the cart to the store. She opens the door and gets in.

"Quentin, I am **miserable**," she says. She is crying.

"What?" says Quentin. He is **surprised**. What is wrong?

"You only care about the car," says Rashel.

"That's not true," says Quentin.

"You don't help me do anything," says Rashel.

"I do! I care about you," says Quentin.

"If you care about me, sell this car," says Rashel.

CHAPTER 2
Going to A Meeting / telling time

STORIA

Thomas lascia il suo condominio. È una bella giornata. Il sole splende. L'aria è fresca. Thomas ha un incontro importante oggi. Thomas è il CEO di una società. Oggi si incontra con nuovi investitori. Egli è preparato per l'incontro. Si sente rilassato.

Sono le otto in punto del mattino. Thomas cammina lungo la strada della città. È in anticipo. Vuole del **tempo** in più. Non vuole essere in ritardo. Non vuole essere stressato.

Thomas vive in una grande città. Ci sono edifici alti ovunque. I taxi passano. Ci sono molte auto. A Thomas piace camminare. A volte prende la metro.

Thomas vuole fare colazione. Si ferma in un bar. Il bar è tranquillo. La musica suona. Thomas vuole qualcosa da mangiare.

"Cosa desidera?" chiede il barista.

"Un muffin, per favore", dice Thomas.

"Mirtillo o cioccolato?" chiede il barista.

"Mirtillo, per favore", dice Thomas.

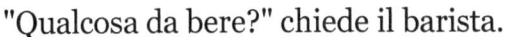

"Qualcosa da bere?" chiede il barista.

"Un caffè", dice Thomas.

"Espresso?" chiede il barista.

"No, macchiato ", dice.

"Da portare via?" chiede il barista. Thomas guarda il suo orologio. **Sono le otto e mezza**. Ha tempo.

"Lo prendo qui," dice Thomas. Si siede e mangia. Guarda la gente camminare. Thomas guarda di nuovo il suo orologio. Sono le nove in punto. Si alza. Thomas getta la spazzatura e va in bagno. Si toglie l'orologio per lavarsi le mani. Il suo orologio è d'oro e non gli piace bagnarlo. Il suo telefono suona.

"Ciao", dice Thomas.

"Signore, è in ufficio?" chiede la segretaria di Thomas.

"Non ancora", dice Thomas. "Sto arrivando."

Lascia la caffetteria. Thomas cammina verso la metropolitana. Ha tempo, quindi non ha bisogno di un taxi. Guarda di nuovo l'orologio. Ma il suo orologio non c'è. Thomas va in panico. Ripensa alla mattinata. Lo ha lasciato a casa? No. Ricorda di essersi tolto l'orologio e di essersi lavato le mani. L'orologio è rimasto al bar.

Thomas torna al bar.

"Mi scusi", dice al barista.

"Ha trovato un orologio d'oro?" chiede.

"Solo un secondo", dice il barista. Chiede ai suoi colleghi. Nessuno ha l'orologio.

"No," dice il barista. Thomas va in bagno. Guarda intorno al lavandino. L'orologio non c'è. Qualcuno ha preso l'orologio, Thomas pensa. Non ha più tempo per cercarlo.

"Mi scusi", dice di nuovo al barista.

"Che ora è?" chiede.

"Sono le dieci e zero nove" dice il barista.

"Grazie", dice Thomas. Thomas si affretta. Ha la riunione ad un quarto alle undici. Si precipita alla fermata della metropolitana. C'è una lunga fila per acquistare i biglietti. Aspetta per cinque **minuti**.

"Sa dirmi che ore sono?" chiede Thomas a una donna.

"Sono le dieci **e mezza**", dice. Thomas è in ritardo. Lascia la lunga fila. Va in strada. Fa segno a un taxi. Tutti i taxi sono pieni. Infine, un taxi si ferma. Thomas entra nel taxi.

"Dove andiamo?" chiede l'autista.

"Tra la 116esima e il parco", dice Thomas.

"Ok", dice l'autista.

"Per favore, sbrighiamoci", dice Thomas. "Devo essere **puntuale** per una riunione."

"Sì, signore", dice l'autista.

Thomas arriva in ufficio. Esce dal taxi e sale le scale. La sua segretaria lo saluta. Thomas è sudato!

"Signore, la riunione è **tra un'ora**", dice il segretario. Thomas si asciuga il sudore dalla faccia.

"Bene", dice Thomas. Si prepara per l'incontro. La sua camicia è sudata. Puzza. Thomas decide di comprare una nuova camicia per l'incontro.

Thomas va al negozio in fondo alla strada.

"Salve, signore", dice il venditore. "Come possiamo aiutarla?"

"Ho bisogno di una nuova camicia", dice Thomas. Il venditore porta Thomas a vedere le camicie. Ci sono camicie rosa, camicie marroni, camicie a schacchi e camicie a quadri. Il venditore parla molto. Thomas è nervoso per l'orario.

"**Che ore sono?**" chiede Thomas il venditore.

"**È quasi mezzogiorno**", dice il venditore.

"Ok," dice Thomas. "Mi dia la camicia marrone." Il venditore porta la camicia marrone alla cassa. Il venditore piega la camicia e **si prende il suo tempo.**

Il telefono di Thomas squilla. È sua moglie.

"Tesoro, ceniamo alle sette **di sera**", dice.

"Ok, cara", dice Thomas. "Non posso parlare adesso."

"Ok", dice. "Non voglio che torni a casa alle nove **sta sera**."

"Non preoccuparti", dice Thomas.

"Ciao", dice sua moglie. Thomas riaggancia il telefono.

"Mi scusi", dice Thomas. "Ho fretta. Non ho bisogno che la camicia sia incartata."

"Va bene," dice il venditore. Thomas paga e lascia il negozio. Si cambia la camicia mentre cammina per strada. La gente lo guarda. Si affretta verso l'ufficio.

"**È ora**," dice la sua segretaria quando entra. Stanno aspettando nella sala riunioni. Gli investitori si siedono intorno al tavolo. Thomas li saluta.

"Mi piace la tua camicia, Thomas", dice uno degli investitori.

"Grazie", dice Thomas. "È nuova." Thomas abbassa il telefono e accende il suo computer.

"Grazie per essere venuti", dice Thomas. "Ho preparato una presentazione. Dura circa quindici minuti."

Thomas si rivolge alla sua segretaria. "Che ora è?"

"**Sono le dodici e un quarto**", dice.

"Grazie", dice Thomas. "Ho perso il mio orologio."

"Perché non guardi il telefono per l'orario?" dice uno degli investitori.

"Certo", dice Thomas. È così abituato al suo orologio che dimentica di poter guardare il telefono per l'ora!

"Devo essere l'ultima persona al mondo ad usare solo l'orologio per **sapere l'ora**", dice Thomas. Tutti ridono.

RIASSUNTO

Thomas inizia la sua giornata molto in anticipo. fà colazione e si rilassa. Va in bagno e lascia il suo orologio in bagno. Quando si rende conto, torna al bar. L'orologio è scomparso. Ora deve chiedere a tutti che ora è. Arriva in ritardo in ufficio. Fortunatamente, il suo incontro è rinviato di un'ora. Va a comprare una nuova camicia. Ci vuole più tempo del previsto. Si precipita alla riunione. Quando chiede l'ora, si rende conto che potrebbe semplicemente guardare il suo telefono per sapere l'orario. La riunione inizia.

LISTA DI VOCABOLI

Sono le......in punto	It is ____ o'clock
Del mattino	in the morning

Tempo	time
..e mezza	half past ___
In punto	on the dot
Secondo	second
Che ore sono	What time is it?
Zero	oh
Del mattino	a.m.
...meno un quarto	a quarter to
Minuti	minutes
Sai che ore sono?	Do you have the time?
In tempo	on time

Tra un ora	in an hour
Che ora è?	What's the time?
Quasi	nearly
Mezzogiorno	noon
Predere il suo tempo	takes her time
Di será	p.m.
Della será	at night
È ora	about time
Dura…. minuti	minutes long
Sapere l'ora	tell the time

www.LearnLikeNatives.com

DOMANDE

1) Perché Thomas perde l'orologio?

    a) Si stacca

    b) Lascia che un estraneo lo tenga

    c) Fa una scommessa

    d) Se lo toglie per lavarsi le mani

2) Dove vive Thomas?

    a) in una piccola città

    b) in una città con pochi mezzi di trasporto

    c) in una grande città

    d) in campagna

3) Thomas è fortunato perché:

    a) ha dei colleghi simpatici

    b) la sua riunione è rinviata

    c) la metropolitana non è affollata

    d) non perde l'orologio

4) Thomas dice al venditore di non incartare la camicia perché:

    a) è in ritardo per la sua riunione

    b) il sudore sulla camicia puzza

    c) sua moglie aspetta al telefono

    d) odia sprecare carta

5) Tutti ridono alla fine della storia perché:

    a) La camicia di Thomas è sudata

b) Thomas è imbarazzato

c) Thomas dimenticava che si può guardare l'ora dal telefono

d) Thomas perde l'orologio.

RISPOSTE

1) Perché Thomas perde l'orologio?

    d) Se lo toglie per lavarsi le mani

2) Dove vive Thomas?

    c) in una grande città

3) Thomas è fortunato perché:

    b) la sua riunione è rinviata

4) Thomas dice al venditore di non incartare la camicia perché:

a) è in ritardo per la sua riunione

5) Tutti ridono alla fine della storia perché:

c) Thomas dimenticava che si può guardare l'ora dal telefono

www.LearnLikeNatives.com

Translation of the Story

Going to A Meeting

STORY

Thomas leaves his apartment building. It is a beautiful day. The sun shines. The air is fresh. Thomas has an important meeting today. Thomas is the CEO of a company. Today he meets with new investors. He is prepared for the meeting. He feels relaxed.

It is **eight o'clock in the morning**. Thomas walks down the city street. He is early. He wants extra **time**. He does not want to be late. He does not want to stress.

Thomas lives in a big city. There are tall buildings everywhere. Taxis drive by. Lots of cars drive by.

Thomas likes to walk. Sometimes he takes the subway.

Thomas wants to eat breakfast. He stops at a café. The café is relaxed. Music plays. Thomas wants a baked good.

"What would you like?" asks the barista.

"A muffin please," says Thomas.

"Blueberry or chocolate?" asks the barista.

"Blueberry, please," says Thomas.

"Anything to drink?" asks the barista.

"A coffee," says Thomas.

"Black?" asks the barista.

"No, with a bit of cream," he says.

"To go?" asks the barista. Thomas looks at his watch. It is **half past eight.** He has time.

"For here," says Thomas. He sits down and eats. He watches people walk by. Thomas looks at his watch again. It is nine o'clock **on the dot**. He gets up. Thomas throws out the trash and goes to the bathroom. He takes off his watch to wash his hands. His watch is gold and he doesn't like to get it wet. His phone rings.

"Hello," says Thomas.

"Sir, are you at the office?" asks Thomas's secretary.

"Not yet," says Thomas. "I'm on my way."

He leaves the coffee shop. Thomas walks towards the subway. He has time, so he doesn't need a taxi. He looks at his watch again. But his watch is not there. Thomas feels panic. He thinks back over the morning. Did he leave it at home? No. He remembers taking off the watch and washing his hands. The watch is at the coffee shop.

Thomas runs back to the coffee shop.

"Excuse me," he says to the barista.

"Do you have a gold watch?" he asks.

"Just a **second**," says the barista. He asks his colleagues. No one has the watch.

"No," says the barista. Thomas goes to the bathroom. He looks by the sink. The watch is not there. Someone has the watch, Thomas thinks. He has no time to look any more.

"Excuse me," he says to the barista again.

"**What time is it?**" he asks.

"**Ten oh nine a.m.**" says the barista.

"Thanks," says Thomas. Thomas hurries. He has the meeting at a quarter to eleven. He rushes to the subway stop. There is a long line to buy tickets. He waits for five **minutes**.

"Do you have the time?" Thomas asks a woman.

"It's ten **thirty**," she says. Thomas is late. He leave the long line. He goes to the street. He waves for a taxi. All the taxis are full. Finally, a taxi stops. Thomas gets into the taxi.

"Where are you going?" asks the driver.

"To 116th and Park," says Thomas.

"Ok," says the driver.

"Please hurry," says Thomas. "I need to be **on time** for a meeting."

"Yes, sir," says the driver.

Thomas arrives to the office. He runs out of the taxi and up the stairs. His secretary says hello. Thomas is sweaty!

"Sir, the meeting is now **in an hour**," says the secretary. Thomas wipes the sweat off his face.

"Good," says Thomas. He prepares for the meeting. His shirt is sweaty. It smells bad. Thomas decides to buy a new shirt for the meeting.

Thomas goes to the store down the street.

"Hi, sir," says the salesperson. "How can we help you?"

"I need a new dress shirt," says Thomas. The salesperson takes Thomas to see the shirts. There are pink shirts, brown shirts, checked shirts, and plaid shirts. The salesperson talks a lot. Thomas is nervous about the time.

"**What's the time?**" Thomas asks the salesperson.

"It's **nearly noon**," says the salesperson.

"Ok," says Thomas. "Give me the brown shirt." The salesperson takes the brown shirt to the cash register. She folds the shirt. She **takes her time**.

Thomas's phone rings. It is his wife.

"Honey, we have dinner at seven **p.m.**," she says.

"Ok, dear," says Thomas. "I can't really talk right now."

"Ok," she says. "I just don't want you to come home at nine o'clock **at night**."

"Don't worry," says Thomas.

"Bye," says his wife. Thomas hangs up the phone.

"Excuse me," says Thomas. "I'm in a hurry. I don't need the shirt wrapped."

"Ok," she says. Thomas pays and leaves the store. He changes his shirt as he walks down the street. People stare. He hurries to the office.

"It's **about time**," says his secretary when he walks in. They are waiting in the meeting. The investors sit around the table. Thomas says hello.

"I like your shirt, Thomas," says one of the investors.

"Thanks," says Thomas. "It is new." Thomas sets his phone down and turns on his computer.

"Thank you for coming," says Thomas. "I have a presentation. It is about fifteen minutes long."

Thomas turns to his secretary. "What time is it?"

"It is **twelve fifteen**," she says.

"Thanks," says Thomas. "My watch is missing."

"Why don't you look at your phone for the time?" says one of the investors.

"Of course," says Thomas. He is so accustomed to his watch that he forgets he can look at the phone for the time!

"I must be the last person in the world to only use a watch to **tell the time**," says Thomas. Everyone laughs.

www.LearnLikeNatives.com

CHAPTER 3
Lunch with The Queen / to be, to have + food

STORIA

Ursula **è** una giovane ragazza. Vive a Londra, in Inghilterra. Studia a scuola. Ama cucinare. **Ha** un'ossessione: la famiglia reale. Vuole **essere** una principessa.

Una sera, Ursula è a casa. Sua madre prepara la cena. Hanno qualcosa di nuovo. Sua madre porta il piatto a tavola.

"Cosa **sono** quelli?" chiede Ursula.

"Questi sono **porri**", dice la mamma di Ursula.

"Oh, non mi piacciono i porri", dice Ursula.

"Provali", dice la mamma. Ci prova. Quasi vomita.

"Quasi sto male", dice Ursula.

"Che esagerata", dice sua madre.

"Per favore, dammi qualche altra verdura," dice Ursula. "**Carote, broccoli, insalata?**"

"Oh, Ursula, mangia la tua **carne** allora", dice sua madre. Accende la televisione. Guardano il telegiornale. Il servizio parla della Regina d'Inghilterra. Ursula smette di mangiare. Presta molta attenzione.

"La regina Elisabetta regna in Inghilterra da 68 anni," dice il notiziario. "È sposata con il principe Filippo. Hanno quattro figli."

Il notiziario parla della Regina. Vive a Buckingham Palace. È molto in salute, nonostante la sua età.

"Voglio visitare Buckingham Palace", dice Ursula.

"Sì, cara", dice sua madre. Guardano il programma. Il programma annuncia una gara speciale. Una persona può vincere una visita a Buckingham Palace. Il vincitore **pranzerà** con la regina. Ursula urla.

"**Devo** vincere!" esclama.

"Non lo so", dice sua madre. "Molte persone partecipano al concorso."

Ursula guarda il programma. Impara come partecipare. Si fa una foto mentre mangia. Poi la pubblica sui social media. Lei guarda il programma, che parla del pranzo con la regina. Lei guarda mentre parlano di ciò che è successo a un principe del Sud Pacifico.

La Regina è su una barca con il principe. Servono il **dessert**. Il principe dimentica di guardare la Regina. Prende **dell'uva** e delle **ciliegie** dalla **frutta** sul tavolo e le mette nella sua ciotola. Gli versa sopra la **panna**. La cosparge di **zucchero**. Inizia a mangiare, e poi si rende conto che la regina non ha ancora iniziato. Fa un grosso errore.

www.LearnLikeNatives.com

La regina prende il suo cucchiaio. Lei mangia un po'. Questo fa sentire meglio il principe. È molto imbarazzato.

"Ci sono delle regole per mangiare con la Regina?" chiede a sua madre.

"Certo", dice sua madre.

"Ad esempio?" chiede Ursula.

"Beh, la Regina inizia il pasto e finisce il **pasto**", dice la mamma di Ursula.

"Non puoi mangiare finché non lo fa lei", dice Ursula.

"Proprio così", dice sua madre. "E quando finisce, finisci anche tu."

"E se non hai finito?" chiede Ursula.

"Hai finito lo stesso," dice sua madre. "E devi aspettare che la Regina si sieda."

"Prima di sederti?" dice Ursula.

"Esatto", dice sua madre. Ursula ci pensa. Ci sono un sacco di regole se sei regina o principessa. Ursula e sua madre finiscono la cena e vanno a dormire.

La mattina dopo, Ursula si sveglia. È nervosa per il concorso. Oggi annunciano il vincitore. Fa **colazione** con sua madre.

"Sono nervosa", dice.

"Ursula, non vincerai", dice sua madre. "Ci sono così tante persone in gara."

"Oh", dice Ursula. È triste. Mangia i suoi **cereali**. Non ha fame. **Pancetta** e **uova** restano intatte.

Accendono la televisione.

"E annunciamo il vincitore di "A pranzo con la Regina", dice l'uomo alla TV. Mette la mano in un'enorme urna di vetro piena di bigliettini.

Muove la mano. Tira fuori un biglietto. Apre il biglietto.

"E il vincitore è... Ursula Vann!" dice.

Ursula guarda sua madre. Sua madre la guarda.

"L'hai sentito?" chiede. Sua madre annuisce, con gli occhi sbarrati. La sua bocca è aperta.

"Ho vinto?" chiede. Sua madre annuisce, senza parole.

"Woo-hoo!" grida Ursula. "Sapevo che avrei vinto! Vedrò la regina!" Ursula finisce il suo cibo e va a scuola.

Il giorno dopo è il giorno del pranzo con la regina. Ursula cammina fino al palazzo. È terrorizzata. È solo una giovane ragazza. Questa è una grande avventura per una ragazza così giovane.

"Chi sei?" chiede una guardia.

"Ursula Vann," dice. "Ho vinto il concorso per pranzare con la Regina."

"Oh, buongiorno, signorina," dice la guardia. "Sei una giovane ragazza carina. Entra pure."

"Grazie", dice lei.

Una guardia la porta al palazzo. È maestoso, e molto grande. Camminano attraverso le sale. La guardia ha un cappello bizzarro. Ursula ridacchia. Poi, si ferma. Sono nella sala da pranzo.

La Regina d'Inghilterra è seduta a tavola! C'è un piatto di **panini** davanti a lei. È minuta. È contenta e sorride.

"Ciao, cara", dice.

"salve, **Vostra Maestà**," dice Ursula. E fa un inchino.

"Grazie per essere venuta a pranzo", dice.

"È un piacere, Vostra Maestà", dice Ursula.

"Spero non vi dispiaccia. Prenderemo il tè invece di un pranzo completo", dice la Regina. Si siede di nuovo. Ursula ricorda il protocollo. E si siede anche lei.

I panini sono panini reali, pensa. Assomigliano molto ai panini di casa, però. Alcuni hanno **prosciutto** e **formaggio**, con un po' di **senape** gialla. Altri hanno sopra un'insalata di **maionese**. C'è un piatto di biscotti accanto ad alcune focaccine.

"Perdonatemi, Vostra Maestà", dice Ursula.

"Sì, cara?" disse la Regina.

"Cosa c'è in quel panino?" chiede.

"Oh, questa è la mia preferita", dice la Regina. "Panino con **insalata** di porri."

"Oh, porri," dice Ursula. Si sente male. La Regina ne prende uno e da un morso.

"Prendine uno, cara", dice la Regina.

"Grazie, Vostra Maestà", dice Ursula. Prende un panino al porro. Può sentire il suo stomaco sottosopra. Fa un morso enorme perché è molto nervosa. La sua faccia diventa bianca, poi verde.

"Va tutto bene, cara?" chiede la Regina. "Sembra tu stia molto male."

"Sto bene," dice Ursula. Sente il suo stomaco girare. Si sente come se dovesse vomitare. Non può impedire ai porri di tornare su per la gola. Almeno ha seguito le altre regole per pranzare con la regina, pensa. Nessuno ha mai detto nulla riguardo a vomitare.

RIASSUNTO

Ursula è una giovane ragazza. Vive a Londra, in Inghilterra. È ossessionata dalla famiglia reale. Cena con sua madre e guarda la TV. In TV, annunciano un concorso. Il vincitore può andare a pranzo con la regina. Ursula si iscrive. Il giorno dopo, a colazione, annunciano il vincitore. È Ursula! Va a pranzo a Buckingham Palace. Lei segue le regole per mangiare con la regina. La regina ha preparato panini speciali. Purtroppo, l'insalata di porri non è il cibo preferito di Ursula. Ursula si sente male mentre mangia il panino ai porri offerto dalla Regina.

LISTA DI VOCABOLI

È	is
Ha	has
Essere	to be
Avere	have
Loro sono	They are
Porri	leeks
Io sono	I am
Verdura	vegetable

Carota	carrot
Broccoli	broccoli
Insalata	salad
Pranzo	lunch
Dovere	have to
Dessert/dolce	dessert
Uva	grapes
Ciliege	cherries
Frutta	fruit
Panna	cream
Zucchero	sugar

Pasto	meal
Colazione	breakfast
Cereali	cereal
Uova	egg
Pancetta	bacon
Panini	sandwiches
Tè	tea
Prosciutto	ham
Formaggio	cheese
Senape	mustard
Biscotti	cookies

www.LearnLikeNatives.com

Facaccine	scones
Insalata	salad

DOMANDE

1) Cosa succede quando Ursula prova i porri per la prima volta?

    a) li ama

    b) sua madre li brucia

    c) quasi vomita

    d) non se ne accorge

2) Qual è la regola quando si mangia con la Regina d'Inghilterra?

    a) non devi mangiare finché non inizia lei

    b) devi indossare il blu

    c) devi mangiare panini

    d) devi sederti prima di lei

3) Cosa pensa la mamma di Ursula del concorso?

    a) Ursula ha possibilità di vincere

    b) è una truffa

    c) la Regina non dovrebbe essere coinvolta

    d) Ursula non vincerà mai

4) Cosa mangia la Regina a pranzo?

    a) un buon arrosto

b) salmone, il suo preferito

c) tè, biscotti e panini

d) è top secret

5) Quale delle seguenti affermazioni è vera?

a) Ursula va via a metà del pranzo

b) Ursula non riesce a controllare la sua reazione ai porri

c) la Regina si è fatta i panini da sola

d) i panini non sono un cibo adatto per un pranzo

RISPOSTE

1) Cosa succede quando Ursula prova i porri per la prima volta?

c) quasi vomita

2) Qual è la regola quando si mangia con la Regina d'Inghilterra?

a) non devi mangiare finché non inizia lei

3) Cosa pensa la mamma di Ursula del concorso?

d) Ursula non vincerà mai

4) Cosa mangia la Regina a pranzo?

c) tè, biscotti e panini

5) Quale delle seguenti affermazioni è vera?

b) Ursula non riesce a controllare la sua reazione ai porri

Translation of the Story

Lunch with The Queen

STORY

Ursula **is** a young girl. She lives in London, England. She studies at school. She loves to bake. She **has** an obsession: the royal family. She wants **to be** a princess.

One night, Ursula is at home. Her mother prepares her dinner. They **have** something new. Her mother brings the plate to the table.

"What **are** those?" asks Ursula.

"These are **leeks**," says Ursula's mom.

"Oh, I don't like leeks," says Ursula.

"Try them," says her mom. She tries them. She almost vomits.

"I **am** sick," says Ursula.

"No, you are not," says her mom.

"Please, give me any other **vegetable**," says Ursula. "**Carrots, broccoli, salad**?"

"Oh, Ursula, just eat your **meat** then," says her mom. She turns on the television. They watch the news. The report is about the Queen of England. Ursula stops eating. She pays close attention.

"Queen Elizabeth reigns in England for 68 years," says the news report. "She is married to Prince Phillip. They have four children."

The news report talks about the Queen. She lives in Buckingham Palace. She is very healthy, despite her age.

"I want to visit Buckingham Palace," says Ursula.

"Yes, dear," says her mom. They watch the program. The program announces a special competition. One person can win a visit to Buckingham Palace. The winner will eat **lunch** with the queen. Ursula screams.

"I **have to** win!" she shouts.

"I don't know," says her mom. "Many people enter the contest."

Ursula watches the program. She learns how to enter. She takes a picture of herself eating. Then she posts it on social media. She watches the program, which talks about eating with the Queen. She watches as they show what happened to a prince from the South Pacific.

The Queen is on a boat with the prince. They serve **dessert**. The prince forgets to watch the Queen. He takes some **grapes** and some **cherries** from the **fruit** on the table and puts them in his bowl. He pours **cream** over them. He sprinkles **sugar** on top. He starts to eat, and then he realizes the Queen has not. He makes a big mistake. The Queen takes her spoon. She eats a bit. That makes the prince feel better. He is very embarrassed.

"There are rules to eat with the Queen?" she asks her mom.

"Of course," says her mom.

"Like what?" asks Ursula.

"Well, the Queen begins the **meal** and ends the meal," says Ursula's mom.

"You mean you can't eat until she does," says Ursula.

"That's right," says her mom. "And when she finishes, you finish, too."

"What if you aren't finished?" asks Ursula.

"You are," says her mom. "And you must wait for the Queen to sit."

"Before you sit?" says Ursula.

"Right," says her mom. Ursula thinks about this. There are lots of rules if you are queen or princess. Ursula and her mom finish dinner. They go to sleep.

The next morning, Ursula wakes up. She is nervous about the contest. Today they announce the winner. She eats **breakfast** with her mom.

"I am nervous," she says.

"Ursula, you won't win," says her mom. "So many people are in the contest."

"Oh," says Ursula. She is sad. She eats her **cereal**. She is not hungry. Her **bacon** and **eggs** sit untouched.

They turn on the television.

"And we announce the winner of the Lunch with the Queen Contest," says the man on the TV. He puts his hand into a huge glass bowl full of papers. He moves his hand around. He pulls out a paper. He opens the paper.

"And the winner is…Ursula Vann!" he says.

Ursula looks at her mom. Her mom looks at her.

"Did you hear that?" she asks. Her mom nods, staring. Her mouth is open.

"Did I win?" she asks. Her mom nods, speechless.

"Woo-hoo!" shouts Ursula. "I knew I would! I'm going to see the queen!" Ursula finishes her food and goes to school.

The next day is the day for lunch with the Queen. Ursula walks up to the palace. She is terrified. She is only a young girl. This is a big adventure for such a young girl.

"Who are you?" asks a guard.

"Ursula Vann," she says. "I won the contest to have lunch with the Queen."

"Oh, hello, young lady," the guard says. "You are a pretty young lass. Come in."

"Thank you," she says.

A guard takes her to the palace. It is grand, and very big. They walk through the halls. The guard has a funny hat. Ursula giggles. Then, she stops. They are in the dining room.

The Queen of England is sitting at the table! There is a plate of **sandwiches** in front of her. She is small. She is happy, and she is smiling.

"Hello, dear," she says.

"Hello, your majesty," Ursula says. She courtsies.

"Thank you for coming to lunch," she says.

"It is my pleasure, your **Majesty**," says Ursula.

"I hope you don't mind. We will be having **tea** instead of a proper lunch," says the Queen. She sits again. Ursula remembers her manners. She sits, too.

The sandwiches are royal sandwiches, she thinks. They look a lot like sandwiches from home, though. Some have **ham** and **cheese**, with a yellow bit of **mustard**. Others have a **mayonnaise** salad on them. There is a plate of **cookies** next to some **scones**.

"Pardon me, your Majesty," says Ursula.

"Yes, dear?" says the Queen.

"What is on that sandwich?" she asks.

"Oh, that's my favorite," says the Queen. "Leek **salad** sandwich."

"Oh, leeks," says Ursula. She feels sick. The Queen reaches for one. She takes a bite.

"Have one, dear," says the Queen.

"Thank you, your Majesty," says Ursula. She takes a leek sandwich. She can feel her stomach turn. She takes a huge bite because she is so nervous. Her face turns white, then green.

"Are you alright, dear?" asks the Queen. "You look quite unwell."

"I- I- I'm fine," says Ursula. She feels her stomach turning. She feels as if she will vomit. She can't stop the leeks from coming back up her throat. At least she followed the other rules for eating lunch with the Queen, she thinks. Nobody ever said anything about vomiting.

CONCLUSION

You did it!

You finished a whole book in a brand new language. That in and of itself is quite the accomplishment, isn't it?

Congratulate yourself on time well spent and a job well done. Now that you've finished the book, you have familiarized yourself with over 500 new vocabulary words, comprehended the heart of 3 short stories, and listened to loads of dialogue unfold, all without going anywhere!

Charlemagne said "To have another language is to possess a second soul." After immersing yourself in this book, you are broadening your horizons and opening a whole new path for yourself.

Have you thought about how much you know now that you did not know before? You've learned everything from how to greet and how to express your emotions to basics like colors and place words. You can tell time and ask question. All without opening a schoolbook. Instead, you've cruised through fun, interesting stories and possibly listened to them as well.

Perhaps before you weren't able to distinguish meaning when you listened to Italian. If you used the audiobook, we bet you can now pick out meanings and words when you hear someone speaking. Regardless, we are sure you have taken an important step to being more fluent. You are well on your way!

Best of all, you have made the essential step of distinguishing in your mind the idea that most often hinders people studying a new language. By approaching Italian through our short stories and dialogs, instead of formal lessons with just grammar and vocabulary, you are no longer in the 'learning' mindset. Your approach is much more similar to an osmosis, focused on speaking and using the language, which is the end goal, after all!

So, what's next?

This is just the first of five books, all packed full of short stories and dialogs, covering essential, everyday Italian that will ensure you master the basics. You can find the rest of the books in the series, as well as a whole host of other resources, at LearnLikeNatives.com. Simply add the book to your library to take the next step in your language learning journey. If you are ever in need of new ideas or direction, refer to our 'Speak Like a Native' eBook, available to you for free at LearnLikeNatives.com, which clearly outlines practical steps you can take to continue learning any language you choose.

We also encourage you to get out into the real world and practice your Italian. You have a leg up on most beginners, after all—instead of pure textbook learning, you have been absorbing the sound and soul of the language. Do not underestimate the foundation you have built reviewing the chapters of this book. Remember, no one feels 100% confident when they speak with a native speaker in another language.

One of the coolest things about being human is connecting with others. Communicating with someone in their own language is a wonderful gift. Knowing the language turns you into a local and opens up your world. You will see the reward of learning languages for many years to come, so keep that practice up!. Don't let your fears stop you from taking the chance to use your Italian.

Just give it a try, and remember that you will make mistakes. However, these mistakes will teach you so much, so view every single one as a small victory! Learning is growth.

Don't let the quest for learning end here! There is so much you can do to continue the learning process in an organic way, like you did with this book. Add another book from Learn Like a Native to your library. Listen to Italian talk radio. Watch some of the great Italian films. Put on the latest CD from Pavarotti. Take cooking lessons in Italian. Whatever you do, don't stop because every little step you take counts towards learning a new language, culture, and way of communicating.

www.LearnLikeNatives.com

www.LearnLikeNatives.com

www.LearnLikeNatives.com

Learn Like a Native is a revolutionary **language education brand** that is taking the linguistic world by storm. Forget boring grammar books that never get you anywhere, Learn Like a Native teaches you languages in a fast and fun way that actually works!

As an international, multichannel, language learning platform, we provide **books, audio guides and eBooks** so that you can acquire the knowledge you need, swiftly and easily.

Our **subject-based learning**, structured around real-world scenarios, builds your conversational muscle and ensures you learn the content most relevant to your requirements. Discover our tools at ***LearnLikeNatives.com***.

When it comes to learning languages, we've got you covered!

www.ingramcontent.com/pod-product-compliance
Lightning Source LLC
Chambersburg PA
CBHW071741080526
44588CB00013B/2111